POVESTEA NUMERELOR

THE NUMBER STORY

SMALL BOOK ONE

ENGLISH - ROMANIAN

Numbers Teach Children
Their Number Names

written and illustrated by

MISS ANNA

Early Reader Edition of *The Number Story 1*
Bronze Medal Winner, 2016 Wishing Shelf Book Award

Library of Congress Control Number: 2018902040

Names: Miss Anna, author.
Title: Number story : numbers teach children their number names / Miss Anna.
Description: Portland, OR: Lumpy Publishing, 2018.
Identifiers: ISBN 978-1-945977-22-0 | LCCN 2018902040
Summary: The pictures and rhymes present stories which introduce numbers 0-10.
Subjects: LCSH Numeration—English--Romanian--Pictorial works--Juvenile literature. | BISAC JUVENILE NONFICTION /
Languages: English--Romanian
Classification: LCC QA141.3 .M57 2018 | DDC 513—dc23

Publisher: Lumpy Publishing
Website: www.missannabooks.com
Email: missanna@missannabooks.com

Paperback: ISBN 978-1-945977-22-0
Printed in the U.S.A.   1 3 5 7 9 10 8 6 4 2

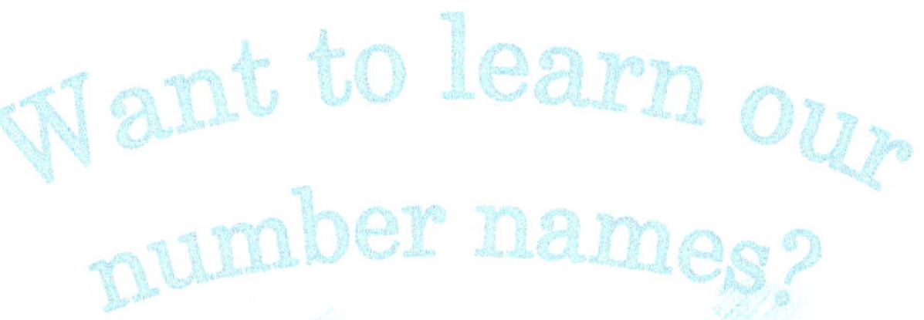

Vrei să înveți numele
Numerelor noastre?

It is very easy and a lot of fun!

E ușor și distractive!

Say-along our little jingle

Cântă cu noi povestioara noastră!

starting from Number One!

Hai să începem de la Numărul Unu!

1

ONE looks like my one finger.

UNU

e ca un degetul meu.

ONE!
UNU!

2

TWO trails a tail.

DOI cară o coadă.

A TAIL! O COADĂ!

3

THREE has bumps.

TREI

are umflături.

BUMPY!   UMFLAT!

4

FOUR carries a sail.

PATRU

cară un pânze.
vele

A SAIL!
O BARCĂ CU PÂNZE!

5

FIVE is a racing track.

CINCI

este o pistă de curse.

VRooM
VRUUUM!
1

SIX curves like a snail.

ȘASE

se curbează ca un melc.

A SNAIL! UN MELC!

7

SEVEN   has a sharp angle.

ȘAPTE

are un unghi ascuțit.

BE CAREFUL! IT'S SHARP!
AI GRIJĂ! ESTE ASCUȚIT!

8

EIGHT   is rollercoaster rails.

OPT

este un montagne russe.

IUPII!
YIPPEE!

NINE is a bubble on a stick.

NOUĂ

este o bulă pe un băț.

A BUBBLE! O BULĂ!

10

TEN   is an eye of a whale.

ZECE

este un ochi a unei balene.

HELLO! BUNĂ ZIUA!

And
ȘI
0
ZERO   is an empty pail.
ZERO
e o găleata goală.

IT'S
EMPTY!
E GOL!

Thank you for playing with us today.

We had a lot of fun too!

Mulțumim că te-ai jucat cu noi azi!

Ne-am distrat de asemenea!

We are your Number friends,
Zero to Ten,
Who will be here for you~
Noi suntem Numerele,
prietenii tăi de la Zero la Zece.
O să fim mereu aici pentru tine.

Bye-bye now!
See you again soon!
Atât pentru acum, la revedere!
O să ne revedem curând!

The Numbers are *SINGING* too!

To sing-a-long, look for Miss Anna Number Story
at your favorite music store like iTUNES.

MP3

Numbers 0-10	Numbers 11-20	Numbers 0-100	About Clocks
IDENTIFYING & COUNTING	& Ordinals	& Place Values	& Telling Time
	first, second, third...	ones, tens, hundreds...	hours, minutes, seconds

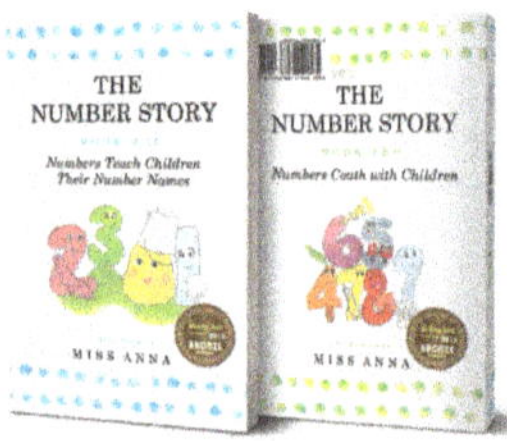

Number Story 1 & 2

isbn: 978-0-996216-48-7

Number Story 3 & 4

isbn: 978-1-945977-01-5

Number Story 5 & 6

isbn: 978-1-945977-06-0

Number Story 7 & 8

isbn: 978-1-949320-40-4

For more Miss Anna books to love,
visit us at

www.missannabooks.com

Numbers are working hard all over the world!
Come Travel the World with Us!

www.ingramcontent.com/pod-product-compliance
Lightning Source LLC
Chambersburg PA
CBHW040859070726
47599CB00035B/2232